For my 4 curly-headed daughters.
Love your curls, girls!

An imprint of Wild Clover Publishing

© Copyright. 2021. Words by Krista Coyne
© Copyright. 2021. Illustrations by Thu Vu

All rights reserved. This book or any portion thereof
may not be reproduced or used in any manner whatsoever
without the express written permission of the author/illustrator
except for the use of brief quotations in a book review.

www.kristacoyne.com

GIRLS with CURLS
The True Tales of Girls with Curly Hair

written by
Krista Coyne

Illustrated by
Thu Vu

In my family, we all have curls.

My mom has curls, my sisters have curls, and even I have some curls.

So we are...

GIRLS WITH

TEAM CURLS!

My mom says it is very important to take care of our curls.
When you comb curly hair you have to be sure to

add this...

and a little of that...

...and don't forget this!

She says our curls are beautiful, and we should wear them proudly.
She said she didn't love her curls until she was old.

Wait! Maybe not *that* old.

The only thing is, whenever mom combs our hair it HURTS!
I can always hear my sisters yelling "OUCH!" no matter where I am in the house.
She always says she's trying her best not to let it hurt, but it still does.

♪ ♫ ♪
la la la

I wonder if it hurts when she combs her own hair.

How does she know how to make so many pretty styles?

When I was really small, mom and dad used to call me "Hair Bear" because I'd wake up with my curls standing on top of my head like this.

Now that I'm older, my hair doesn't seem to have as many curls, but it sure does tangle.

I have a twin sister, but we don't look a lot alike. She has bouncy, spiral curls.

Her hair is so shiny and easier to comb than mine,
but if it's not a school day she won't let my mom touch it.
My mom always tells her how important it is to comb your curls every day.

She gets so mad when my mom reminds her: "It'll be a rat's nest if you don't comb it."

My little sister has lots of super, springy, crazy, curly curls that stick straight up.
No matter what, she always screams when mom brushes her hair –
or even just when mom picks up the brush!

Sometimes her hair can get sooooooo crazy,
looking at it makes me want to say oowww!

one day my little sister decided to cut a chunk of her hair
because she didn't want my mom to comb through the knots.
I didn't think that was such a good idea, but little sisters don't think about that.
of course, we had to take her to the hair salon to fix it,
but even they couldn't cover up the chunk of hair that was missing.

It was so lopsided!

I think she better learn to comb her hair as soon as possible,
or she might end up bald like my dad.

oh my!

My mom tries to keep our hair in place by making us wear night caps to bed.
It kind of feels like you are wearing a shower cap. I don't like it becuase it's so itchy and hot!
Most of the time we wake up with them lying on the pillows next to us, anyway.

One morning,
I woke up with it over my eyes!

Mom buys us all kinds of hair clips and headbands,
but they always seem to pop off and never work.
Well, you know what they say
if your hair looks CRAZY at the end of the day?
Crazy hair equals a crazy day, and ours is crazy every day.

That's why we LOVE when it's "Crazy Hair Day" at school!

All we have to do is wake up and we're ready!

I wish it was "Crazy Hair Day" more than one day a year.

Some days, dad has to do our hair when mom can't.
It takes him soooooo long,
but he doesn't worry about all of the knots like my mom, so we don't mind.
A ponytail on top of our heads is his favorite hairstyle to do.
He tells us we look like beautiful unicorns.

Although curly hair may hurt a little more when you comb it,
I'm starting to see how interesting curls can be.
Almost everyone in my family has curls and they all look different.

So, I'm beginning to think that curly hair is super cool.
No two curly heads are the same.
That means there's never a boring day in the world of curls.
Every day is a different curl.

And I kinda like being unique!

Can you believe it?
My mom and dad told us we are going to have a new baby sister!

I can't wait to see her curls!

About the Author

Krista lives with her husband, four girls, and a big yellow lab named Séamus. When she's not teaching at her local elementary school, she can be found spending time with her kids, crafting, or traveling to Ireland to visit family. Krista started telling stories to her twin girls as she drove them around during the day and rocked them to sleep at night. She quickly started to dream up all kinds of stories from their day-to-day life and finally decided to turn those stories into real books!